We Worship Here

D0297647

Angela Wood & Emma Trithart

W

915 00000214558

Franklin Watts

First published in Great Britain in 2019 by The Watts Publishing Group

Credits
Series Editor: Sarah Peutrill
Series Designer: Anthony Hannant, Little Red Ant

Text consultants:
Religious Education Consultant: Margaret Barratt, Religious Education Lecturer and author
Buddhist Consultant: Dr Desmond Biddulph CBE, President, The Buddhist Society
Reading Consultant: Prue Goodwin, Reading and Language Information Centre, Reading

FSC
www.fsc.org
MIX
Paper from responsible sources
FSC® C104740

ISBN 978 1 4451 6175 4

Printed in Dubai

Franklin Watts
An imprint of
Hachette Children's Group
Part of The Watts Publishing Group
Carmelite House
50 Victoria Embankment
London EC4Y 0DZ

An Hachette UK Company

www.hachette.co.uk
www.franklinwatts.co.uk

Contents

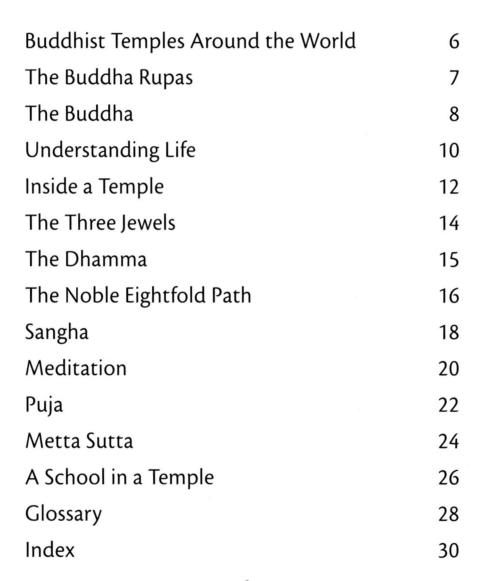

Words in **bold** are in the glossary on page 28.

Buddhist Temples Around the World

A Buddhist temple is a place where Buddhists go to learn about the teachings of the **Buddha**, to show respect for him and to be with other Buddhists.

Some Buddhist temples are called viharas.

There are Buddhist temples all over the world.

THE BUDDHA RUPAS

Buddhists follow the Buddha's teachings but they do not **worship** him as a god. Pictures or images of the Buddha, called Buddha rupas, help Buddhists to remember what the Buddha said and did.

The Buddha's hands are shown in different positions or mudras. Each mudra has a special meaning.

The Buddha

The Buddha was born a prince named Siddattha Gotama. He lived in a palace in Nepal. Siddattha had everything he could want, but he felt that there was more to know about life. He went to see what life was like outside the palace.

There he saw a sick man, an old man and a dead man. He realised that everyone shared the same problem as the three men. Everyone would suffer and die. Siddaattha also saw a monk who was very calm and happy, because he led a peaceful life. Siddaattha decided to leave the palace to seek the answer to finding peace and happiness.

Many temples have paintings showing stories from the Buddha's life, like this scene.

Understanding Life

Siddattha met holy men and tried living their strict and simple lives, but he did not find the answer. Then, one day he decided to sit beneath a tree until he understood why people are unhappy and how they can be really wise, peaceful and happy.

When Siddattha realised the answer he was **enlightened**. Buddha means 'enlightened one' or 'the one who knows'.

A lotus flower grows out of muddy water. The Buddha said becoming 'enlightened' was like growing from muddy water into the light.

Here the Buddha is shown sitting on lotus flowers.

Inside a Temple

Inside a Buddhist temple is a **shrine**. It can be in a special room. The most important part of the shrine is the buddha rupa. It is in the middle and high up to show how special it is. Buddhists place important things all around the Buddha rupa.

Sometimes there is a model of a pointed mound called a **stupa**. When the Buddha died his ashes and some of his belongings were put inside a huge stupa. Now there are reminders of the Buddha and Buddhist writings in stupas.

Here the Buddha sits beneath the bodhi tree where he was enlightened.

A small stupa is in the corner.

The Three Jewels

Three ideas that are important to Buddhists are called the Three Jewels. They are the Buddha, the **Dhamma** and the **Sangha** (the Buddhist community).

Buddha

Dhamma

Sangha

These children are making offerings in front of the Buddha rupa. They say the names of the Three Jewels.

THE DHAMMA

The Dhamma is the name for the Buddha's teachings. The Buddha believed that people cannot be happy if they only think about themselves and their belongings.

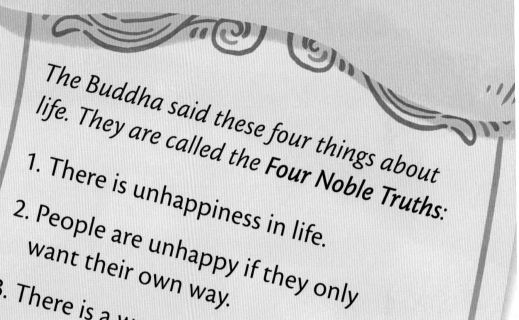

The Buddha said these four things about life. They are called the **Four Noble Truths**:

1. There is unhappiness in life.

2. People are unhappy if they only want their own way.

3. There is a way to end this.

4. The way is called the Noble Eightfold Path. It shows people how to live wisely and happily.

THE NOBLE EIGHTFOLD PATH

The **Noble Eightfold Path** is shown by a wheel with eight spokes. The Noble Eightfold Path is the Middle Way, not too easy and not too hard. It helps Buddhists to be happy by understanding life, doing good things and making their minds peaceful.

This model of the Noble Eightfold Path is on top of a temple. The deer on either side of the model remind Buddhists of a speech the Buddha gave in a deer park.

Sangha

Sangha means all the Buddhist **monks** and **nuns** everywhere. It can also mean the whole Buddhist community. Monks and nuns live a simple life away from their family, just as the Buddha did. They **meditate**, teach the Dhamma and help people. Some do this for their whole lives and others for a short time.

Monks and nuns have very few possessions. They have a robe, bowl, belt, razor, needle, water filter, a toothpick and a walking stick.

Other Buddhists say thank you
to the monks and nuns by giving them food
and sometimes robes. This is called **dana**.

19

Meditation

Meditation is a special kind of thinking. Buddhists meditate to make their minds clear and bright.

Zen Buddhists make special gardens to help them meditate. They have rocks, raked sand or small stones and maybe a few trees.

20

When Buddhists practise meditation they kneel or sit cross-legged, sometimes on cushions, and relax. They sit still and quietly, with their eyes closed or slightly open, and they breathe calmly. Some Buddhists say a verse or **mantra** over and over.

Buddhists meditate in the temple or at home. They meditate on their own or with other people.

PUJA

One way that Buddhists show their respect for the Buddha is through **puja**. They take off their shoes and sit or kneel in front of the shrine. Then Buddhists bow their heads and put their hands together. They say a verse about the Three Jewels:

"I go to the Buddha as my **refuge**.

I go to the Dhamma as my refuge.

I go to the Sangha as my refuge."

They offer flowers to the Buddha. The flowers will die which shows that everything in life changes. They light candles because the Dhamma lights up the world. They burn incense because it has a sweet smell, like the sweetness of the Dhamma, and spreads into the world.

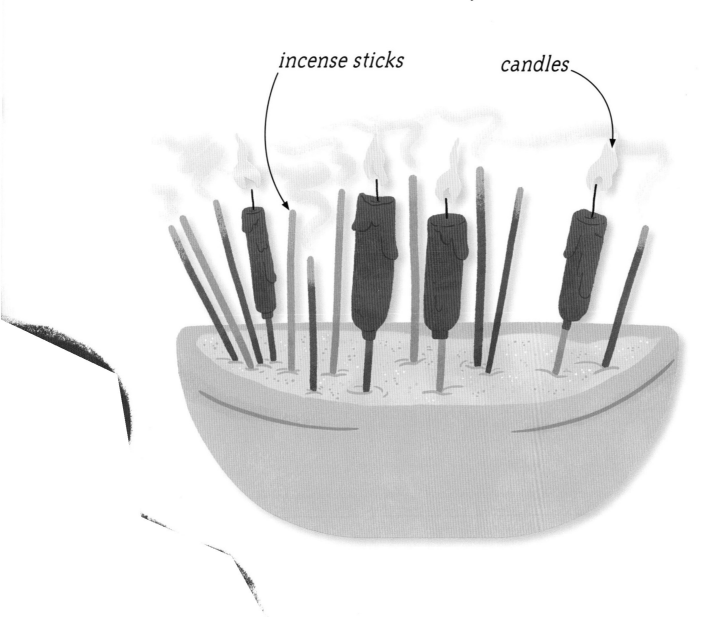

incense sticks

candles

Metta Sutta

The Metta Sutta are verses about loving kindness. At the end of puja the Metta Sutta is often read or chanted. Metta means loving kindness, being peaceful and caring for all living things. The Buddha said that everyone should have metta inside them.

These flags show metta being sent out to everyone and everything in the world.

Buddhists in Tibet turn wheels with mantras on them to send goodness into the world.

25

A School in a Temple

In most Buddhist temples there are classes for children. They learn the Dhamma, often from a monk or nun. They also learn how to meditate and how to lead a Buddhist life.

In the past, the Buddha's teachings along with rules for monks and nuns were written on narrow pieces of palm leaves that were threaded together into books.

What do you think is the most important part of a Buddhist life?

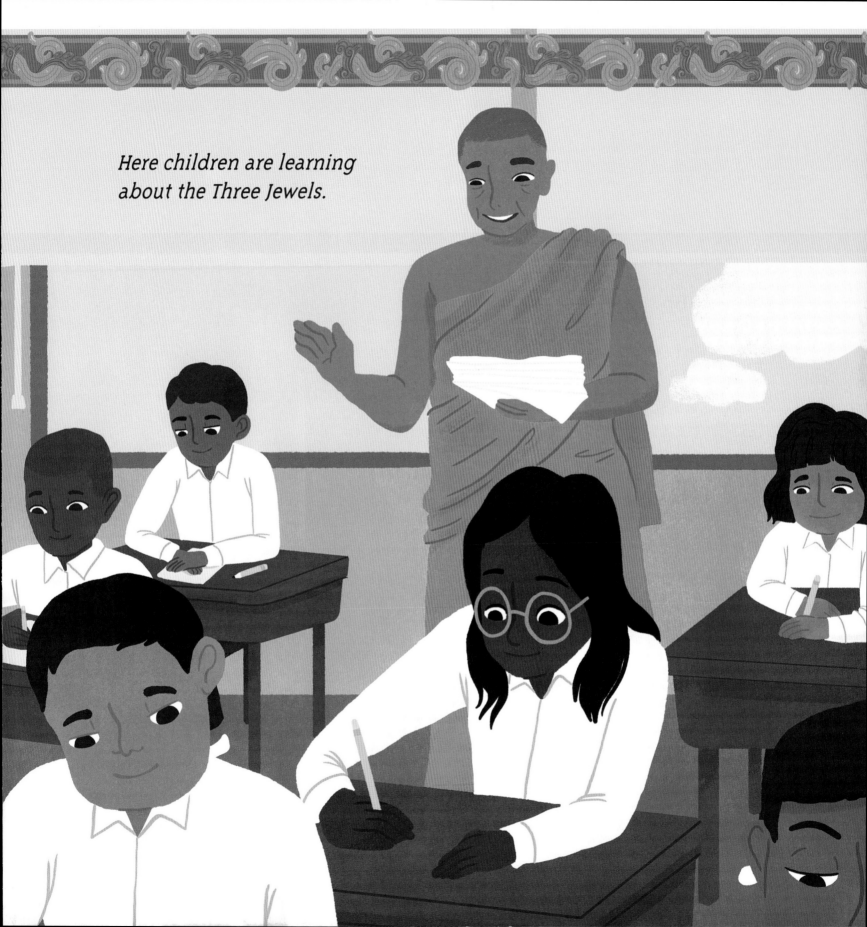

Here children are learning about the Three Jewels.

Glossary

Buddha the 'enlightened one', he was born Siddattha Gotama

dana giving to others who are in need of something, such as clothing or shelter

Dhamma the Buddha's teachings

enlightened seeing things clearly and wisely

Four Noble Truths the four ideas that the Buddha came to understand about suffering and how to end it

mantra a word or phrase that is repeated over and over to calm the mind

meditate to calm your body and make the mind clear

monks men who leave their family to seek enlightenment and teach the Dhamma

Noble Eightfold Path the Buddhist way to find happiness

nuns women who leave their family to seek enlightenment and teach the Dhamma

puja the name of a service and a Buddhist word for showing respect

refuge safety and support

Sangha Buddhist monks and nuns. It can also mean the whole Buddhist community

shrine a Buddha rupa surrounded by offerings

stupa a mound-shaped building in which things to remind Buddhists about the Buddha are kept

worship to show devotion to something you love

Index